for **S.M. Valentine**

Author of the forthcoming:
Sugar Valley: Strip Clubs, Monasteries and Psych Wards.

Deciphering Hemingway's Secret Advice for Writers

Tom Hunter

Indianapolis
Yasnaya Polyana Press
2024

2.0.10

Printed in the U.S.A.
ISBN 978-0-9847559-2-9

Table of Contents

Chapter 1: Introduction

ERNEST Hemingway cast a deep shadow across the 20th Century and beyond. He left his mark on the world of writing and culture. Many writers consider Hemingway the symbol of literary achievement. From the world of writing, to the entirety of Western culture, Papa Hemingway left his mark.

Many budding novelists have pored over the memoir *A Moveable Feast*, over Hemingway's letters and through the shelf of fine biographies written about the man. That experience led many to encounter cryptic bits of advice from Hemingway on the process of writing.

The beginning writer reads that Hemingway said: "Don't describe—invent," and they wonder what that *means*. Likewise, Hemingway often talked about the importance of his "Iceberg Principle". He also said: "Fiction is not interior decorating—it's architecture." Perhaps the most famous bit of advice he gave was: "Write one true sentence". Obviously there is useful advice buried in these cryptic utterances, but how can a writer crack his secrets?

If you have read and re-read every word Mr.

Hemingway wrote in his life—as I have—and likewise consumed the many biographies of the man, you will at first be baffled by the hidden meaning of these phrases.

Hemingway himself alluded to this process in his work *Death in the Afternoon*, where he wrote:

> *"Every novel which is truly written contributes to the total of knowledge which is there at the disposal of the next writer who comes, but the next writer must pay, always, a certain nominal percentage in experience to be able to understand and assimilate what is available as his birthright and what he must, in turn, take his departure from."*[1]

Ernest Hemingway *Death in the Afternoon*

To understand the advice Hemingway left behind for us, we need to read and ponder his words. We find that years later, in a moment of repose or perhaps when we're using a sharp ax to remove an old tree stump, the meaning of Papa's advice comes to us in a flash. These hard-won insights are my gift to you. I understand that you will need to pursue your own journey of discovery to assimilate them as I have, but perhaps I can speed you along by pointing you in the right direction.

In this brief book, I intend to give away the crown jewels of my many decades of deep study and concentration on the life, work and advice of Ernest Hemingway. My goal is to help you learn in a simple and direct manner what I have concluded he meant when he gave these nuggets of advice on writing. I hope that, by the

1 *Death in the Afternoon* by Ernest Hemingway, (1932), Scribners, p.153

end of this book, you will possess the secrets that I have found through decades of study, novel writing and deep reading. My goal is to jumpstart your writing so that you can do as I have tried to do—write books that give as much pleasure to the reader as I have gained from my explorations of the world through books.

Chapter 2: Write One True Sentence

WRITING remains the most paradoxical art. Words are free. Anyone is able to put down on paper any words they want, without limitation. That freedom becomes a chain that prevents the writer from beginning. If everything is equal, where should one begin?

Hemingway spoke early in his career of his method of finding one true sentence and using that as his starting point. Though his advice is concrete, that does not actually lead the writer into useful territory—at least for most of us.

In 1937, Hemingway gave a speech to the American Writer's Conference in New York. In that speech he offered the following insights:

"A writer's problem does not change. He himself changes, but his problem remains the same. It is always how to write truly and, having found what is true, to project it in such a way that it becomes a part of the experience of the person who reads it."[2]

---

2 *Remarks* by Ernest Hemingway, American Writer's Conference,

Since words are all free and any writer can put down any words they want, it makes sense for the writer to chose ones that will be accepted as true by readers. True, here, is interpreted to mean words that are a valid and accurate depiction of life. Unless your desire is to not depict life, then Hemingway's advice makes sense.

When a writer begins the process of trying to write fiction, they find themselves at first struggling to write any words. Then, once some words come, they struggle to comprehend what is that beast called a story? Perhaps they go toward some anecdote that happened to them during their life, or to some great tale they heard. From either beginning point, the result is usually a disappointment. So, every writer faces this question: what is a story?

There are technical explanations of what a story comprises, and most of the understanding of story that existed during Hemingway's time were more of an autopsy of story—seeking to classify the thing after it was written.

The thing that the critic reads is indeed a *story* but the critic dissects a work as if it were dead—a specimen of the story species.

Not especially useful to a writer trying for the first time to write a story.

Also, if you turn to personal experiences, hoping for an idea for a story, anecdotes that happened to you don't really help that much. They generally don't work as stories.

When I attended Iowa State University in my youth —about the same time I fell under Hemingway's spell—I

_____

(1937)

6

took an undergraduate fiction writing class. The professor was someone named Jane Smiley (*before she left academia to become the famous novelist she is today*) and she gave me this advice, which I remembered:

"The events of your story must change the character."

That was sage advice and it leads us to our first great insight. Story is not about a plot—it's about the people in the story. If you as a writer focus only on telling a yarn where the plot is all that matter, readers won't really care.

For a class assignment, I had written a story about a pair of college roommates who had an alley cat they looked after. Thinking I was being clever, I alternated two story lines: one from the point of view of the cat as it lived on the streets, the other from the point of view of the two roommates, who were fighting over whose fault it was the cat had slipped out into the Winter weather.

Jane Smiley told me that she found herself skipping over the cat portions to get back to the roommates. That was my first lesson. The part about the cat was not real—it was not true. The part about the roommates was about people.

So, your first lesson—always keep the people front and center.

As the writer struggles to write a story that keeps the characters in front, they face another, simultaneous problem—the quality of the writing. Since we know that words are effectively free, it's important that we choose the best ones we can and not belabor the reader's attention. When you have written many stories, you come to understand that your job—in the prose that you write—is to provide food for the reader's senses.

In writing circles, this is often summarized with the important: "Show, Don't tell". That's another somewhat cryptic piece of advice that I always consider the embodiment of the idea: "give food for the senses." When a writer does the bad "telling", it's as if the writer were looking through a keyhole at some fascinating scene unfolding. But rather than letting us—the reader—see for ourselves, the bad writer "tells" us a summary of what he is seeing through the keyhole. As readers, we don't want to listen to the writer's bad summary, we want to *see for ourselves*, hear for ourselves, feel what's happening and taste the lemon ourselves.

So, when Hemingway gives us the advice to "write one true sentence", it means that we should give a vivid account of some place or event or feeling. The reader wants the truth—verisimilitude—an accurate representation of the real world.

That advice from me addresses the idea that you must "show not tell", that you must give the reader a first-hand experience of the story. I will revisit this idea in the next chapter, called the "Objective Correlative".

Yet, we have not really explained how to write a story. When I started out I read every book on the writing of fiction. Most were written by literary critics and focused on "theme" and the deeper meaning of the work. The rare books written by fiction writers were aimed at myth making, showing how the author was a genius who received fully-formed novels from her subconscious without working. Joseph Campbell's "The Hero with a Thousand Faces" (1949) was starting down the path of explaining how stories work. Yet again, Campbell was an academic, not a novelist.

Still, there remained a taboo among fiction writers

against spilling the crown jewels on how to write novels.

In 1981, Dean R. Koontz breached this taboo by publishing his book "How to Write Best-Selling Fiction", full of secrets revealed, which he pulled from print and never allowed to be reprinted, for reasons that remain murky to this day.

Stephen King's fine "On Writing" came close to revealing some secrets but his book too is full of hand-waving non-explanations on how he writes stories.

The first systematic book that dissected story in a way useful to novelists was the magnificent "Story Structure Architect" by Victoria Lynn Schmidt.

In this book, we will tease apart Hemingway's secrets.

Chapter 3: The Objective Correlative

THE CONCEPT known as the Objective Correlative was first coined by T.S. Eliot. He said it is: "a set of objects, a situation, a chain of events which shall be the formula of that *particular* emotion." It describes the process where an author refuses to name the emotion that the prose should engender. Instead, the author seeks to *evoke* the emotion by providing specific and significant details that cause the reader to organically *feel* that emotion. It's extremely difficult to achieve but when successful, it provides the greatest writing.

Hemingway called this "the sequence of motion and fact that creates the emotion". This led him to suppress any obvious description of an emotion and to choose an objective relating of the facts of the situation.

For a writer trying to accomplish the same thing, it's certainly best if your original draft can achieve this but I think it's important not to let this need get in the way of writing a story. Also, if you look at the original drafts of Hemingway's work, he does not begin by achieving this sort of effect. He evolves an effective implementation of the principle behind the "objective correlative" through careful and laborious revision.

Hemingway's work is a departure from the fiction of the 19th Century partly because he refuses to spell out the emotion that the reader should take from his fiction. Rightly, I judge, Hemingway looks at that as cheating. The selection of significant details and the flow of the action and dialog must be enough to generate the emotions.

In this respect, Hemingway shares the opinion of the Russian short story and dramatist Anton Chekhov, who believed that "in both scene in character the selection of significant details, grouped so as to convey an image, is the vital thing."[3]

In a later chapter, the example of "Hills Like White Elephants" is given as an example that shows the "Objective Correlative". In that example, as you will read in greater detail there, we see how the final meaning of the story is never overtly stated—yet it is *implied* by what the character does.

This is the hardest kind of writing to do and the most satisfying when the reader grasps the meaning. It makes you feel what is happening rather than being hit over the head with it.

---

3 *Hemingway's Craft* by Sheldon Norman Grebstein, (1973), Southern Illinois University Press, p. 2

"It was a very simple story called 'Out of Season' and I had omitted the real end of it which was that the old man hanged himself. This was omitted on my new theory that you could omit anything if you knew that you omitted and the omitted part would strengthen the story and make people feel something more than they understood."[4]

Ernest Hemingway *A Moveable Feast*

4   *A Moveable Feast* by Ernest Hemingway, (1964), Scribners, p.75

Chapter 4: The Iceberg Principle

ONE OF THE MOST famous of Hemingway's secret pronouncements was his mention, in *A Moveable Feast*, of his Iceberg Principle. This has confused a lot of writers including myself (at first). When you write the original version of a story, you generally know what is going to happen at the end and every word that is written enters the story with that ending in mind. In many cases elements of foreshadowing are given.

In the case of Hemingway's work, there are a multitude of examples where he chose to carve away elements of the story from the final version. However, as he had been writing the story, those carved-away elements left their mark and so the reader *senses* the part that is not stated.

This gives the reader pleasure. It's a greater art to suggest and have the reader understand without being hit over the head with the flat-out description. If the reader reads a story and infers some fact rather than being told it literally, then the reader derives pleasure from being able to sense more than was said.

In his acerbic piece "The Art of the Short Story",

published in The Paris Review, Hemingway tries to clarify what he meant by his "iceberg" theory.

When writing a story, he said, if the writer skips something important—like having a significant event happen out of view, off stage—then the reader thinks: "Wait—what happened?" This is not what Hemingway meant by "iceberg". When significant events occur out of the reader's direct view, it's irritating. It's a hole, a gap, a missing element.

When the writer correctly practices the Hemingway Iceberg, the omission is something the reader will be able t o *infer*. Allowing the reader to close that gap is pleasurable.

Most of what Hemingway wrote in "The Art of the Short Story" sounds like he was drunk when he wrote it. Still, nuggets of insight abound:

"This information is what you call the background of a story. You throw it all away and invent from what you know. I should have said that sooner. That's all there is to writing."

Ernest Hemingway, "The Art of the Short Story".

This brings us closer to what he meant: the writer is *informed* by everything they know about the background of the story. Though all of that background should not be included in the story, its presence is felt in the words that remain, the portion of the iceberg that sticks above the water.

All writing relies on the inclusion of specific, vivid details. However, it's too easy to bog down prose with exposition or other vivid details that don't mean anything.

16

Thus, it's *not enough* to have specific details. They have to be **significant** details. Deciding *which* details are significant constitutes a large part of the job of a fiction writer.

It's the job of an artist to hide their tracks, to remove the scaffolding that allowed them to create great art. So, when Hemingway makes a cut, there are no obvious traces of the omission.

But, if we know what to look for, Hemingway's works are full of examples of the iceberg theory:

The Sun Also Rises

Hemingway's first novel is justly famous and many consider it his greatest work. He wrote the original draft in six weeks. That first draft was not the entire book but just a great start at the whole. Over the course of the following year he expanded and rewrote that first draft.

Budding writers should pay close attention to this sequence of events, because it shows how every writer struggles to get it right.

Hemingway, the writer who at first struggled to write paragraphs, had devoted the entire previous year to writing and perfecting his first novel.

Understand that he worked on that rewrite and polished it *full time* for a year. He said it was the hardest job of rewriting he had ever done.

After that long year of detailed perfectionism, Hemingway felt he had a draft of *The Sun Also Rises* ready to show off. The manuscript was the culmination of everything he knew about writing—it was his best effort.

Through a fortunate meeting with F. Scott

Fitzgerald at this time, Hemingway came to the attention of editor Max Perkins of Scribners.

Fitzgerald had told Max that Hemingway was "the real thing", and that he should take a look at the novel Hemingway had produced.

Before Max Perkins got to see what became *The Sun Also Rises* (TSAR), Fitzgerald did his due diligence and read Ernest's novel himself.

Anyone familiar with the novel's current opening: *"Robert Cohn was once middleweight champion at Princeton..."*, will be shocked by the manuscript Scott Fitzgerald received.

What follows is the original beginning of *Fiesta*, which became *The Sun Also Rises*:

*"Book I
CHAPTER I*

This is a novel about a lady. Her name is Lady Ashley and when the story begins she is living in Paris and it is Spring. That should be a good setting for a romantic but highly moral story. As every one knows, Paris is a very romantic place.

Spring in Paris is a very happy and romantic time. Autumn in Paris, although very beautiful, might give a note of sadness or melancholy that we shall try to keep out of the story. Lady Ashley was born Elizabeth Brett Murray. Her title came from her second husband. She had divorced one husband for something or other, mutual consent; not until after he had put one of those notices in the papers stating that after this date he would not be responsible for any debt, etc. He was a Scotchman and found Brett much too expensive, especially as she had only married him to get rid of him and to get away from home."

Fiesta (The Sun Also Rises), Original opening that Scott

Fitzgerald hated.[5]

After reading that opening, Scott Fitzgerald wrote in a letter filled with dismay that the novel essentially sucked all the way to Chapter 2, until the moment when Hemingway introduced the character Robert Cohn.

"Letter from Scott Fitzgerald to Ernest Hemingway regarding the original opening of The Sun Also Rises.[6]

TRANSCRIBER'S NOTE: Spelling errors are [Fitzgerald's]. Hemingway called [Fitzgerald's] everyday writing illiterate. Nevertheless, I think [Fitzgerald] comes off as quite a lovely and generous person here, and so very unfiltered.

"Dear Ernest: Nowdays when almost everyone is a genius, at least for awhile, the temptation for the bogus to profit is no greater than the temptation for the good man to relax (in one mysterious way or another)—not realizing the transitory quality of his glory because he forgets that it rests on the frail shoulders of professional enthusiasts

This should frighten all of us into a lust for anything honest that people have to say about our work. I've taken what proved to be excellent advice (On the B. + Damned) from Bunny Wilson who never wrote a novel, (on Gatsby—change of many thousand wds) from Max Perkins who never considered writing one, and on T. S. of Paradise from Katherine Tighe (you don't know her) who had probably never read a novel before.
[This is beginning to sound like my own current work

---

5 https://archive.org/stream/sunalsorisesunpublishedopening/SunAlso
Risesfirstchapter#page/n0/mode/2up

6 https://archive.org/stream/sunalsorisesunpublishedopening/SunAlso
Risesfirstchapter#page/n7/mode/2up

which resolves itself into laborious + sententious preliminaries].

Anyhow I think parts of Sun Also are careless + ineffectual. As I said yestiday (and, as I recollect, in trying to get you to cut the 1st part of 50 Grand) I find in you the same tendency to envelope or (and as it usually turns out) to embalm in mere wordiness an anecdote or joke that casually appealed to you, that I find in myself in trying to preserve a piece of "fine writing."

Your first chapter contains about 10 such things and it gives a feeling of condescending casuallness.

"P. 1. "highly moral story" "Brett said" (O. Henry stuff) "much too expensive" "something or other" (if you don't want to tell, why waste 3 wds. saying it.

See P. 23— "9 or 14" and "or how many years it was since 19XX" when it would take two words to say That's what youd kid in anyone else as mere "style" —mere horseshit I can't find this latter but anyhow you've not only got to write well yourself but you've also got to not-do what anyone can do and I think that there are about 24 sneers, superiorities, and nose-thumbings-at-nothing that mar the whole narrative up to P. 29 where (after a false start on the introduction of Cohn) it really gets going.

And to preserve these perverse and willful non-essentials you've done a lot of writing   that honestly reminded of me of Michael Arlen."

F. Scott Fitzgerald, *The Unpublished Opening of The Sun Also Rises*, p.9

Being a good friend, Fitzgerald tried to help Hemingway *repair* the original first two chapters. Hemingway didn't bother to rewrite those first two chapters —he dumped them. Today, the novel comes to us starting *exactly* where Scott Fitzgerald said it started getting good— with the introduction of Robert Cohn.

In the context of the idea of the Iceberg Theory, let's consider the implications of Hemingway's decision. When he performed his year-long rewrite, the bad opening was in place the whole time. Every word he wrote after that followed the "This is a novel about a lady" opening.

So, when he was writing it, he thought the reader would have already read those chapters. Thus, every sentence, paragraph and chapter following that opening was built around *that* opening, with it in mind.

Later, even after he had removed the first 2 chapters, the original opening left its traces. It joined the 7/8ths of the iceberg that existed under water. Not explicitly in the text, but still having its effect.

Thus, according to the Iceberg Principle, it was fine to have removed the opening because it had already left its traces throughout the length of the finished book.

Three Shots, Indian Camp

One of Hemingway's most famous short stories is "Indian Camp", about a doctor performing a caesarian section using a jackknife and tapered gut leader for sutures. This fictional story ends with the Indian husband slitting his own throat—something viewed by the doctor's son Nick.

As the boy Nick and his father ride in canoes back to their own camp, Nick trails his hand in the water and muses that he will never die. Every reader since 1927 has assumed that Nick's reaction to death was just a free-standing reaction to the suicide of the Indian.

In 1972 the book *The Nick Adams Stories* was published posthumously. It contained an unknown pre-story to "Indian Camp" that was given the name "Three Shots". It described a little boy Nick who had been left behind by his father and uncle while they went night-fishing. His father had given him the instructions: "if any emergency came up while they were gone he was to fire three shots with the rifle and they would come right back."[7] Feeling scared of the night, fearing he would die—even though he was not actually in danger—Nick fired the three shots and recalled his father and uncle. When those two arrived, they found Nick safely asleep.

Hills Like White Elephants

This famous and quite brief story appears to concern a couple who in a railway saloon having and argument about something which is never overtly stated. The reader understands that the man wants the woman to do something and that she is bitter about his request. In this story, you understand that he thinks her doing this unstated thing will restore their relationship. For her, however, the fact that he has even asked her to do this thing has already spoiled the relationship and even if she complies with his request, they would be finished.

The story ends without saying what she has chosen to do. Hemingway never tells us what to think about this story—but just the same we feel what she is going to do.

"Oh yes. But I don't care about me. And I'll do it and then everything will be fine."
"I don't want you to do it if you feel that way."

---

7   *The Nick Adams Stories by Ernest Hemingway*, (1972), Scribners, p.3

The girl stood up and walked to the end of the station. Across, on the other side, were fields of grain and trees along the banks of the Ebro. The shadow of a cloud moved across the field of grain and she saw the river through the trees.

"And we could have all this," she said. "And we could have everything and every day we make it more impossible."

"What did you say?"

"I said we could have everything."

"We can have everything."

"No, we can't."[8]

Ernest Hemingway *The Short Stories of Ernest Hemingway*

In terms of Hemingway's "Iceberg Principle", the hidden part is the subject of this story: abortion. The man wants the woman to get an abortion and she does not want to have one. Yet, the power of the story is undiminished even though we lack this information.

Another point that we have discussed is pertinent to this passage—the "Objective Correlative". Though Hemingway does not come out and tell us what the woman plans to do, he implies it. On one side of the train tracks are barren "hills like white elephants". On the other side are lush wheat fields.

Since the woman pays more attention to the lush wheat fields, this story has generally been interpreted to mean that she does *not* have the abortion. That is the emotion, according to the "Objective Correlative", that the reader is supposed to grasp.

---

8   The Short Stories of Ernest Hemingway by Ernest Hemingway, (1927), Scribners, p.276

The Killers

In his mention of how he wrote "The Killers", Hemingway clearly shows how the Iceberg Principle entailed a thorough understanding of the background and then a willingness to venture into invention.

"Gene Tunney, who is a man of wide culture, once asked me, 'Ernest, wasn't that Andre Anderson in 'The Killers'?' I told it was and that the town was Summit, Illinois, not Summit, N.J. We left it at that. **I thought about that story a long, long time before I invented it**, *and I had to be as far away as Madrid before I invented it properly. That story probably had more left out of it than anything I ever wrote."*

Ernest Hemingway "The Art of the Short Story" (Emphasis added)

The statement I have highlighted is a profound summary of the Iceberg Principle.

"Don't describe—invent."

Hemingway himself considered one of his stories, "A Clean Well-Lighted Place", to be the pinnacle of this technique of omission.

A Clean Well- Lighted Place

This spare story omits the back story of every character, and yet we fully understand what each represents: our cast of characters is three.

The old man, piling up saucers as he achieves his nightly drunk, knows his better days are behind him. We know nothing of his situation other than he is rich enough to get drunk, and that his niece cares for him.

The young waiter is impatient and scornful of the old man. We do not know why only that he is against the old man. Then, we have the other waiter, who knows that he himself will follow the old man into a lonely, desperate end. We feel the fear of onrushing death, the irritation of youth tired of waiting, and the dread of knowing that creeping reality of decline. All these feelings are sensed and nothing is explicitly said.

"*I was trying to write then and I found the greatest difficulty, aside from knowing truly what you really felt, rather than what you were supposed to feel, and had been taught to feel, was to put down what really happened in action;* what the actual things were which produced the emotion that you experienced. *In writing for a newspaper you told what happened and, with one trick and another, you communicated the emotion aided by the element of timeliness which gives a certain emotion to any account of something that has happened on that day;* but the real thing, the sequence of motion and fact which made the emotion *and which would be as valid in a year or in ten years or, with luck and if you stated it purely enough, always, was beyond me and I was working very hard to try to get it.*"

Ernest Hemingway "Death in the Afternoon"

This gets at the root: "what the actual things were which produced the emotion that you experienced" and then "the real thing, the sequence of motion and fact which made the emotion". He is never, ever, telling us what or how to feel. Hemingway always encodes and embeds his meaning in concrete details.

Big Two-Hearted River

This short story by Hemingway has been famous since it was first published for the quality and depth of the description. It has only one character, Nick Adams, and he seems to be fighting against anxiety for a reason that is not clear from a surface reading of the story.

However, there are clues that Nick had formerly loved fishing this river but that some events that have happened in his recent past have interfered with his happiness. Given the history of Nick Adams, as portrayed in a variety of stories that came before "Big Two-Hearted River", the reader comes to understand that Nick has come back from the war and that he is suffering from what we now call "post-traumatic stress syndrome" (PTSD).

The war is not mentioned at all in the story but Nick's anxiety is apparent throughout. A slight problem that he encounters with landing a big fish sets him off. Nick's happiness in his fishing seems much more fragile than it should be: "he had not been unhappy all day... Nothing could touch him"[9].

This is yet another example of the Iceberg Principle. As Hemingway wrote this story, he knew the *reason* for his anxiety but he scrupulously kept a specific description of the event [shell shock] out of the story.

Remember *A Moveable Feast*:

---

9 *The Short Stories of Ernest Hemingway* by Ernest Hemingway, (1927), Scribners, p.215

"This was omitted on my new theory that you could omit anything if you knew that you omitted and the omitted part would strengthen the story and make people feel something more than they understood.... When I stopped writing I did not want to leave the river where I could see the trout in the pool, its surface pushing and swelling smooth against the resistance of the log-driven piles of the bridge. The story was about coming back from the war but there was no mention of the war in it."[10]

Ernest Hemingway A Moveable Feast

One of the most recently published books on the subject of Ernest Hemingway is the book *Hemingway's Boat: Everything He Loved in Life, and Lost, 1934-1961,* by Paul Hendrickson.

The author suggested that Hemingway may have got his first inkling of the power of the iceberg principle by his practice of writing abbreviated cables in his journalism for the Toronto Star.

"The pull and sport of telegram expression, in which the sender seeks to relay as much information as possible in as few words as possible, went back for him to at least 1922, when, having just been elevated to a staff reporter, he was wiring dispatches about the Greco-Turkish war from Constantinople to his penny-pinching bosses at the Toronto Star.

As the great literary historian Malcolm Cowley once wrote, cable-ese for Hemingway 'was an exercise in omitted everything that can be taken for granted,' which is another way of understanding how he arrived at his literary method."[11]

---

10 *A Moveable Feast* by Ernest Hemingway, (1964), Scribners, p.75-76

11 *Hemingway's Boat* by Paul Hendrickson, (2011), Knopf, p.86

Paul Hendrickson *Hemingway's Boat*

Among the multitude of jewels in *A Moveable Feast*, Hemingway describes himself working out of cafes in Paris, and how his imagination hitched a ride on a young lady who entered the cafe.

This passage gives his best description of living to write and the process of flow, when the story seems to write itself or is gently coaxed along.

"*A girl came in the café and sat by herself at a table near the window. She was very pretty with a face fresh as a newly minted coin if they minted coins in a smooth flesh with rain-freshened skin, and her hair was black as a crow's wing and cut sharply and diagonally across her cheek.*

I looked at her and she disturbed me and made me very excited. I wished I could put her in the story, or anywhere, but she had placed herself so she could watch the street and the entry and I knew she was waiting for someone. So I went on writing. **The story was writing itself** *and I was having a hard time keeping up with it.*

...

*"I've seen you, beauty, and you belong to me now, whoever you are waiting for and if I never see you again, I thought. You belong to me and all Paris belongs to me and I belong to this notebook and this pencil. Then I went back to writing and I **entered far into the story and was lost in it. I was writing it now and it was not writing itself and I did not look up nor know anything about the time nor think where I was nor** order any more Rum St. James."*[12]

Ernest Hemingway *A Moveable Feast*

---

12 A Moveable Feast by Ernest Hemingway, (1964), Scribners, p.6

War & Peace

The greatest example of the Iceberg Principle is embodied in *War & Peace*, the book itself.

Tolstoy, over in Russia, began writing what became "War & Peace" in 1863—when the American Civil War was about half over.

Dipping a quill pen in an inkwell, newly married Leo was 35 years old when he began writing "War & Peace", a process that would require six years and seven complete, from scratch, drafts.

Unlike most other authors, a draft was not a trifling word-smith of the manuscript for Tolstoy. Writing another draft mean another draft starting over from fresh imagination, without referring to the last draft. He invented it anew, each draft tearing through the compromises and imprecision of the last draft.

The first draft is published in English. It clocks in at 912 pages. The final draft is 1,370 pages. What is the difference?

The book itself sprang from Tolstoy's desire to write a historical epic—but for every event in Russia's history, there was always an antecedent event, and another and another.

At first, Tolstoy thought to write about the 1825 Decembrist uprising, but then he ended up starting instead in 1805. During the six years and seven drafts that Tolstoy wrote Война и мир, he was newly wed to Sonya, 18 years his younger. She managed the estate and have Lev the luxury of scribbling on his book in the mornings, then spending the afternoon hunting. Sonya was busy running the estate all day and the she ended her night by reviewing Leo's latest writings. Most importantly, she made a fair copy of his work every night—finishing sentences that were fragments, making comments about the story.

Then, each morning, Leo started with her fair copy, and went on with his story.

All this is background to our purpose—which is to show how *Tolstoy himself* practiced the Iceberg Theory. The first version of what became W&P was a more surface exploration of the subject of the Napoleonic wars from both the war and home sides. But, after he finished with what he wanted to cover in his book, he read his prose and decided that there were nuances he didn't get around to covering.

So, unlike most writers, Tolstoy did not get at the greater depth of meaning that he desired by tweaking and word-smithing is previous draft. No, Tolstoy set that long and hard fought draft aside, and started from the beginning again, not referring to his previous draft—only from memory.

Tolstoy followed this same process, of slaving away he and Sonya to finish a draft—only to have him change his mind and think "I can do better."

Tolstoy was not finished with "War & Peace" until he had finished 7 (VII, 0111, *seven*) drafts—each and every one from scratch—with a feather quill pen that he had to dip in an ink well. The first draft of the book is published in English, as is the final draft, obviously.

All of the drafts themselves were published in Russian between 1928 and 1958, in volumes 13-16 of the Jubilee Edition of Tolstoy's complete works.

Each prior version included insights and evolutions in the manuscript that show no trace in the final except as filtered through Tolstoy's unique mind.

Chapter 5: "Don't Describe, Invent"

GENERALLY, if you are a beginning writer, you try to write a story about interesting things that happened to you. You describe those events as vividly as you can, giving the details, the dialog as best you remember it and the settings exactly as they were. Invariably, the result is flat, lifeless and a pale imitation of what they remembered. One could consider the result as a useless pile of wasted words but in fact there is one good outcome from this exercise—that experience is used up. Most likely, the writer will consider that experience a bad try and move on to some other personal experience.

The best that can be expected from these writing attempts is a pile of failed story attempts that are lifeless and boring at worst, flat and uninspiring in the best cases. The entire exercise is essential and of critical importance to the nascent writer. Why? Writing them digs them out of the writer's head and gets them out of the way of the deeper personal experiences that are beneath them. Still, if those stories are based on real life experiences, they will be flat and useless exercises.

Back to the title of this chapter: "Don't Describe, Invent": whenever you write a story that is based heavily on something you personally experienced, your imagination remains tethered to the real events that happened to you. You never stray from the boundaries of the real event that you experienced. The story will never fly higher than your real and "true" experiences because that is what inspired it.

But doesn't that conflict with Hemingway's edict to "write one true sentence"? No, not at all. When you write a story based on real-life experiences, you "describe" the real things that happened to you. When you imagine something brand new that happened to you, the process is "invention". The writer makes up the story, the characters and the scenes out of imagination. Your imagination is free to fly and go anywhere because you are living a brand new experience at the time of your writing.

Inside the posthumous book *The Nick Adams Stories* was a section that had originally been included in "Big Two-Hearted River". Hemingway deleted this section before publication but it's relevant to this discussion.

"Writing about anything actual was bad. It always killed it. The only writing that was any good was what you made up, what you imagined. That made everything come true. Like when he wrote 'My Old Man' he'd never seen a jockey killed and the next week George Parfrement was killed at that very jump and that was the way it looked. Everything good he'd ever written he made up. None of it ever happened. Other things had happened. Better things, maybe. That was what the family couldn't understand. They thought it all was experience."[13]

Ernest Hemingway *The Nick Adams Stories*

---

13 *The Nick Adams Stories* by Ernest Hemingway, (1972), Scribners, p.246

Hemingway yet again refers to his process in the section of *A Moveable Feast* where he discusses Scott Fitzgerald and his practice of altering the endings of his stories to make them suitable for the *Saturday Evening Post*, which was Scott's cash cow.

"I could not believe this and I wanted to argue him out of it but I needed a novel to back up my faith and to show him and convince him, and I had not yet written any such novel. Since I had started to break down all my writing and get rid of all facility and try to make instead of describe, writing had been wonderful to do. But it was very difficult, and I did not know how I would ever write anything as long as a novel. It often took me a full morning of work to write a paragraph."

Ernest Hemingway *A Moveable Feast* (1964), p.154

Consider the long quote from *A Moveable Feast* that heads this chapter. Hemingway wrote: "The story was writing itself". That happens when you invent. You *live in the story* as you write. As you write, in your mind you are the character and you are living the scene—you're inventing it as you write. Hemingway wrote: "*I entered far into the story and was lost in it.*" This is the precise thing that happens when you invent.

If your character is a Russian Mafia kingpin named Vladimir Szlotov—who is killing people in the story—then while you *write* it you yourself *are* Vladimir Szlotov and *you* are dragging the man Pokcha's head through a

33

bandsaw.[14]

If your character is a little Russian girl named Galina Yosheva who is terrified as she is being chased into the sewers in St. Petersburg, then *you are terrified* in the story as you write her flight. You invent the story as you write it by living it. How do you write scary fiction? You invent characters who are *themselves* terrified.

A common nugget of advice for writers is: "write what you know". That leads naive writers to think their job is writing about their own life. Quite the opposite: it means "live the story you are writing" or, to interpret Hemingway's advice: "Don't describe—*invent*". Don't describe things that have already happened to you, invent new ones—imagine them and write down what you experience as you imagine.

When you get good at invention, you can sometimes steer the story and that is what Hemingway meant when he said: ***"I was writing it now and it was not writing itself"***. He became so adept at invention that he can do what any writer deep in invention can do: rudder the story in directions your story needs. The general practice I have found works best is starting a chapter with a beat or two you would like to accomplish. Then, live in the story and look for an opportunity to pounce on the story points you had wanted to accomplish. That does not always work—often the story takes you where it wants to go—and you should let it. Invention tasks the best part of your imagination and you should allow that work to happen.

In his posthumous work *The Garden of Eden*, the main character David Bourne—who is a writer—amplifies this idea:

---

14 *The Butcher of Leningrad* by Tom Hunter, (2013), Antenna Books.

*"The story had not come to him in the past few days. His memory had been inaccurate in that. It was the necessity to write it that had come to him. He knew how the story ended now. He had always known the wind and sand scoured bones but they were all gone now and he was **inventing** all of it. It was all true now because **it happened to him as he wrote** and only its bones were dead and scattered and behind him. It started now with the evil in the shamba and he had to write it."[15]*

Ernest Hemingway *The Garden of Eden* (1986), p.93-94

This is the most insightful advice I have found in Hemingway: you invent by living in the story. If you follow that process, I am confident you will be able to write your story well.

"When writing a novel a writer should create living people; people not characters. A character *is a caricature. If a writer can make people live there may be no great characters in his book, but it is possible that his book will remain as a whole; as an entity; as a novel. If the people the writer is making talk of old masters; of music; of modern painting; of letters; or of science then they should talk of those subjects in the novel. If they do not talk of those subjects and the writer makes them talk of them he is a faker, and if he talks about them himself to show how much he knows then he is showing off.*

No matter how good a phrase or simile he may have if he puts it where it is not absolutely necessary and irreplaceable he is spoiling his work for egotism.

"Prose is architecture, not interior decoration, and the

---

15 *The Garden of Eden* by Ernest Hemingway, (1986), Scribners, p.93-94

Baroque is over. For a writer to put in his own intellectual musings, which me might sell for a low price as essays, into the mouths of artificially constructed characters which are more remunerative when issued as people in a novel is good economics, perhaps, but does not make literature. People in a novel, not skilfully constructed characters, *must be projected from the writer's assimilated experience, from his knowledge, from his head, from his heart and from all there is of him.*"[16]

Ernest Hemingway *Death in the Afternoon*

---

16 *Death in the Afternoon* by Ernest Hemingway, (1932), Scribners, p.153

Chapter 6: "Fiction is architecture, not interior decorating"

THE STATEMENT that Hemingway made is less opaque than many of his other nuggets of advice on writing. In short, this means that it isn't enough to write in a beautiful way, one that gives food for the senses —though that is also required. Hemingway here is referring to a reality that every budding writer needs to understand: what is a story?

During the time when Hemingway lived and until the present day, many books have been written that attempt to define this question—what is a story. However, in virtually all cases, they approach the question in a forensic manner, trying to understand why a given story works and how. They seek to give a definition for what story is in the abstract. These explanations do not give the writer who approaches a blank paper an idea of how to proceed. The beginning writer needs a plan that suggests to them how they should start writing.

In 1981, Dean Koontz wrote a long-out-of-print book called, variously, "How to Write Best-Selling Fiction". There is a lot of market advice in this book that is now antiquated but there are many nuggets that are seriously golden. I had been on a quest to understand the question: "What is a story?" from the perspective of someone starting to write a story and on page 75 of Mr. Koontz's book, I found the answer:

The Classic Plot

"The vast majority of successful novels share the same story pattern. I have boiled this pattern down to four steps, and although this is somewhat simplistic, it is essentially accurate:
1) *The author introduces a hero (or heroine) who has just been or is **about to be plunged into terrible trouble**.*
2) *The hero attempts to solve his problem but only slips into deeper trouble.*
3) *As the hero works to climb out of the hole he's in, complications arise, each more terrible than the one before, until it seems as if his situation could not possibly be blacker or more hopeless than it is—and then one final, unthinkable complication makes matters even worse. In most cases, these complications arise from mistakes or misjudgments which result from the interaction of the faults and virtues that make him a unique character.*
4) *At last, deeply affected and* changed *by his awful experiences and by his intolerable circumstances, the hero learns something about himself or about the human condition in general, a Truth of which he was previously ignorant, and having learned this lesson, he understands what he must do to get out of the dangerous situation in which he has wound up. He takes the necessary actions and either*

succeeds or fails, through he succeeds more often than not, for readers tend to greatly prefer fiction that has an uplifting conclusion "[17].

Dean Koontz *How to Write Best-Selling Fiction*

The sentence about "plunged into terrible trouble" was the eureka moment for me. That taught me how to start a story. Each person's definition of "terrible trouble" is different, too. As you cast about for stories to write, keep in mind this idea of terrible trouble.

You need a character who has been plunged into terrible trouble. Also, most critically, the trouble must have happened to your main character. It cannot be trouble that occurred to her son or to his father—it must be trouble that directly affects the main character. Now, let's take a moment to understand what is meant by that term "main character". These are important questions about architecture that Hemingway is referring to without ever explaining. In a story, there are concepts such as the "main character" and the "protagonist". The main character is the person who represents the reader in the story. The reader views the story through the eyes of the main character. The protagonist, on the other hand, is the person whose actions move the story forward. If the story has been written in the first person, then the main character and the protagonist are one and the same person. In terms of "terrible trouble", it is the main character who must have been plunged into terrible trouble. That means the reader—who identifies with the main character—has been plunged into terrible trouble. When seeking to answer that all important question of "what is a story"—which is a question about the

---

17 *How To Write Best-Selling Fiction* by Dean Koontz, (1981), Writer's Digest Books, p.75

architecture of the story—we're really asking: "What trouble has the main character been plunged into?"

Shakespeare's Plots

That question—what is a story—has plagued writers going back to the time of the ancient Greeks and even to writers such as William Shakespeare. For example, a German named Gustav Freytag noticed that the five-act plays of Shakespeare pretty much follow one plot structure: Introduction, Growth, Climax, Fall, Catastrophe. These five sections of the bard's plays have distinct architectural roles to play, which we shall review.

1) The "Introduction" introduces the *complication* o r *inciting incident*— something we have described as the original "terrible trouble". This is the origin of the conflict that will drive the story through to the end. When this conflict is completely resolved, the story must end.

2) Growth, or rising action, this is the series of events that complicate things. Koontz described this as the worst possible thing that could have happened on top of the inciting incident.

3) The Climax—this is the turning point of the story, the central event that happens and sets the main character on an inescapable course to the end.

4) The Fall—these are the events that follow as an inevitable result of the climax.

5) The Catastrophe is the final conclusion—the ending that comes as a response to the

climax. This completes the circle.

Sounds pretty clear on the surface, right?

But often we hear a modern reader describe a novel or even a filmgoer describe a film, saying the "climax" at the end was exciting. From the dramatic structure of Shakespeare's plays, we know the climax really does not come at the end of the story—it comes in the precise center.

Let's consider a real-life example. If I enter a tavern and walk up to the barmaid and, out of the blue, slap her face—that's pretty "climactic", right? But is that the end of it? Nope! No story is complete until we see *her reaction.* She's going to hit me back and then we're even.

The same idea occurs in Shakespeare's plots, with the five-act play Macbeth providing a great example.

In Act I, the *Introduction,* the three witches appear in a storm. They tell Macbeth that—if three things happen, he will become king.

In Act II, the *Growth,* the current King Duncan comes to visit Macbeth and Macbeth decides he's going to kill him. Macbeth kills King Duncan and the murder is discovered. The identity of the killer is not known and Macbeth is crowned King. Banquo suspects Macbeth.

In Act III, the *Climax,* Banquo is himself killed.

In Act IV, *Fall,* Banquo's ghost appears and the reality that the killer is Macbeth becomes generally known. Lady Macbeth dies.

In Act V, *Catastrophe,* they come and murder Macbeth for the murder of King Duncan. So, the idea to take from this is that for centuries plot structure has been about architecture—about completing the movement of a story. This is part of the architecture that Hemingway was referring to and, as you can see, understanding this is a huge undertaking.

The complexities inherent in the architecture of

fiction are huge and they must be understood.

Take another example—what is the general difference between a Tragedy and a Comedy?

In a Tragedy: you think they're going to win, you think they're going to win—they lose.

In a Comedy: you think they're going to lose, you think they're going to lose—they win.

As you can see, it's the reversal at the end that completes the dramatic structure. So, the nature of the ending is embedded in the architecture of the story all along —and if the author decides to change that—it's artificial and false.

Take the famous example of Charles Dickens' serial novel *The Old Curiosity Shop*. This novel was published first in weekly installments, over 88 weeks. It is a chase story. In the beginning, Little Nell and her Grandfather are running away from the loan shark Quilp.

The novel is the story of the gradual success of the pursuit. Since this was published in 88 weekly serial installments, Dickens required almost two years to publish the entire thing, and his readers had not choice but to live with him in the story as he wrote it.

Along the way, Dickens had followed this pattern: "you think they're going to win, you think they're going to win" and guess what? About 3/4ths of the way through the book—with the last 1/4th still to be written—his best friend John Forster observed: "You know you're going to have to kill her, don't you." The conclusion of the story is implicit throughout the novel and had Dickens not observed that reversal—he would not have completed his structure. Dickens had no choice but to kill Little Nell at the end. Indeed, there is a famous true story of crowds of American readers of Dickens' episodic serial novel *The Old Curiosity*

Shop crowding on to the piers, shouting out to the crews of ships just in from England the question: "Is Little Nell dead?"[18] (She was.)

Hemingway said rightly that fiction is not interior decoration—but architecture. These examples from Shakespeare and Dickens give examples of that fact.

So, when you create your own novel, you must make sure to finish your story. When you deliver a novel to your agent, she will look to make sure that you have taken all your story lines to their true conclusions—their catastrophes. Each of the subplots too must be taken to their catastrophes. Finish the stories.

*"[Gertrude Stein] had also discovered many truths about rhythms and the **uses of words in repetition** that were valid and valuable and she talked well about them."*

Ernest Hemingway *A Moveable Feast* (1964), p.17

---

18 The Old Curiosity Shop by Charles Dickens, (1840), Chapman & Hall, eBookEden edition p. 11

Chapter 7: The Uses of Repetition

IN MOST academic writing, one is advised to pull out the thesaurus and vary the words used to provide variety and *avoid* repetition. In reality, there are times when a skilled author such as Ernest Hemingway intentionally uses repetition in the service of parallelism and to provide a chiming effect that increases the power of the writing. This effect can be seen all through Hemingway's oeuvre but most of all it is apparent in his youthful writing.

Take the example of his first real story "Up in Michigan", the same one Gertrude Stein chided for being *inaccroachable*, a word Stein coined and meant the story was unpublishable because it contained indiscrete mentions of lascivious behavior. In "Up in Michigan" we see the most transparent example of Hemingway's repetition:

*"Liz **liked** Jim very much. She **liked** it the way he walked over from the shop and often went to the kitchen door to watch for him to start down the road. She **liked** it about his mustache.*

*She **liked** it about how white his teeth were when he smiled. She **liked** it very much that he didn't look much like a blacksmith. She **liked** it how much D.J. Smith and Mrs. Smith **liked** Jim. One day she found that she **liked** it the way the hair was black on his arms and how white they were above the tanned line when he washed up in the washbasin outside the house. **Liking** that made her feel funny.*

Ernest Hemingway *The Short Stories of Ernest Hemingway* (1927), p.81

Obviously, the repetition here concerns the word "liked". This example is not as effective as later examples because it draws attention to itself. However, sometimes the more obvious examples clue the student into the practice that becomes more artfully hidden in later works.

The most famous example of repetition by Gertrude Stein herself comes in her 1922 poem "Sacred Emily" which contains the line: "A rose is a rose is a rose." Based on the seemingly pointless repetition in her *magnum opus* "The Making of Americans", it appears that Gertrude Stein had a great idea in repetition that she was not able to use effectively.

In Hemingway's earliest stories, he tries to get away with more repetitions but the deeper we go into his writing, the more judiciously he uses it.

In the story "On the Quai at Smyrna", he still does not have the repetition perfectly calibrated and it is not as powerful as it will become.

"The strange thing was, he said, how they screamed every night at midnight. I do not know why they screamed at that time. We were in the harbor and they were all on the pier and at

46

midnight they all started screaming."

Ernest Hemingway The Short Stories of Ernest Hemingway (1927), p.87.

In most later examples, Hemingway learns to limit his repetitions—or chiming—to only two or three times. The effect is to magnify the power of the writing.

Take this example from the Nick Adams story that first appeared in Hemingway's tremendous first collection *In Our Time*, "The Doctor and the Doctor's Wife":

> *"Now, Doc—"*
> *"Take your stuff and get out."*
> *"Listen, Doc."*
> *"If you call me Doc once again, I'll knock your eye teeth down your throat."*
> *"Oh, no, you won't, Doc."*
> *Dick Boulton **looked** at the doctor. Dick was a **big man**. He knew how **big** a **man** he was. He liked to get into fights. He was happy. Eddy and Billy Tabeshaw leaned on their cant hooks and **looked** at the doctor. The doctor chewed the beard on his lower lip and **looked** at Dick Boulton."*

Ernest Hemingway *The Short Stories of Ernest Hemingway* (1927), p.101

The effect is subtle and powerful. It makes the prose circle again and again, getting stronger with every repetition.

The earliest examples of his repetition were limited to a single word but as he grew in maturity and experience, he used repetition of phrases and even whole sentences, as

Grebstein noted in his monograph *Hemingway's Craft*:

"There is the basic repetition of a key word or phrase, together with subtle in emphasis and hints of new meanings.... Another type is syntactical repetition, wherein Hemingway aligns several phrases or clauses of similar grammatical structure in a sequence, again with small incremental modifications. Or, he may expand the repetition into a rhetorical pattern by building it into a series of like sentences, perhaps with identical openers. Or, he may combine one or more of these methods into a single intricate design running to paragraph length and beyond."[19]

Sheldon Norman Grebstein, Hemingway's Craft (1973), p. 134-135

A later example of the subtle uses of repetition comes in *The Old Man and the Sea* where the incantation of "I wish I had the boy with me" or its variations is repeated over and over. By using this simple sentence, Hemingway calls to the reader's attention the entire beginning of the novel where we met the boy and understood that the old man's bad luck had taken even the boy away from him.

Tolstoy

Hemingway himself describes a series of writers that he metaphorically boxed with and beat but there is one who he refused to even get in the metaphorical boxing ring

---

19 *Hemingway's Craft* by Sheldon Norman Grebstein, (1973),
   Southern Illinois University Press, p. 134-135

with, and that is Leo Tolstoy.

Hemingway mentioned several writers who inspired him and, as his student, I went on to read the complete works of all the writers he admired such as Ivan Turgenev and Leo Tolstoy. There are several examples of how Tolstoy effectively demonstrates the power of repetition without drawing attention to the artifice.

The first example is in his *Sevastopol Sketches*—specifically the first: "Sevastopol in December", which has the following, amazing passage:

"On a bed on the other side of the chamber you will see the pale, tortured, delicate face of a woman, both her cheeks alight with the red glow of fever. 'This is the wife of one of our sailors, sir; she was hit in the leg when a shell landed near her on the fifth,' your guide informs you.

"'On her way to the bastion with her husband's dinner, she was, when it happened.'

"'So, what do they do, amputate?'

"'Yes, sir, they sawed off her leg above the knee.'

"Now, if you have strong nerves, go through the doorway on the left: that is the room in which wounds are bandaged and operations performed.

There **you** **will** **see** *surgeons with pale, gloomy physiognomies, their arms soaked in blood up to the elbows, deep in concentration over a bed on which a wounded man is lying under the influence of chloroform, open-eyed as in a delirium, and uttering meaningless words which are occasionally simple and affecting. The surgeons are going about the repugnant but beneficial task of amputation.* **You will see** *the sharp, curved knife enter the white, healthy body;* **you will see** *the wounded man suddenly regain consciousness with a terrible, harrowing shrieked cursing;* **you will see** *the apothecary assistant fling the severed arm into a corner;* **you will see** *another wounded man who is lying on a stretcher in the same*

*room and watching the operation on his companion, writhing
and groaning less with physical pain than with the psychological
agony of apprehension; you will witness fearsome sights that
will shake you to the roots of your being; you will see war not as
a beautiful, orderly, and gleaming formation, with music and
beaten drums, streaming banners and generals on prancing
horses, but war in its authentic expression—as blood, suffering
and death."*

Leo Tolstoy *The Sevastopol Sketches*, (1855), p.47-48.
(Translation by David McDuff..)

This remains one of the most harrowing passages I
have ever read, especially when you are reading along and
suddenly this onslaught comes at you in waves. The
repetition itself makes it like a series of visual impressions
that cannot be escaped. The power of this passage, even in
this translation by David McDuff, is profound.

My love of Hemingway led me to read everything
by Tolstoy, led me to learn Russian and led me to live in
Russia myself for a year in 1997. Those experiences
formed the core of three of my works:[20] For my Russian
experiences, I have both Mr Hemingway and *Gospodin*
Tolstoy to thank.

Though Tolstoy's work is replete with examples of
powerful repetition, I will present two more, both from
Tolstoy's most amazing book *War&Peace*[21].

---

20 **The Butcher of Leningrad** (a thriller), **Beelyet (The
Ticket)** (a thriller) and **Dispatches from St. Petersburg** (a
memoir).
21 *Note: if you don't read Russian then the only English
translation you should bother with is the one by Louise Maude.
Emphatically avoid the one by Constance Garnett as she was
sloppy and rushed through her translations. Choose the Inner*

*"Nicholas Rostov meanwhile remained at his post, waiting for the wolf. **By the way** the hunt approached and receded, **by the cries** of the dogs whose notes were familiar to him, **by the way** the voices of the huntsmen approached, receded, and rose, he realized what was happening at the copse. He knew **that** young and old wolves were there, **that** the hounds had separated into two packs, **that** somewhere a wolf was being chased, and **that** something had gone wrong"*

Leo Tolstoy *War & Peace*, (Translated by Louise Maude, Inner Sanctum Ed., 1942), p.550.

These chapters of *War & Peace*, "The Wolf is Taken", remain among the most vivid writing in the book. I encourage you to please read them in their entirety to get the full effect.

But, hopefully, you can see how the power comes from the carefully controlled repetition. This is the model that taught Hemingway, from my best guess. Once you see how Tolstoy handles dynamic parallelism, you see what carefully controlled repetition means and why it is used.

Well, there you have it. This is what Hemingway meant, by my reckoning. Thank you for this conversation.

—Tom

Sanctum edition if you can find one.

www.ingramcontent.com/pod-product-compliance
Lightning Source LLC
Chambersburg PA
CBHW070828100426
42813CB00003B/536